the
vibrant table

wholesome recipes from a food stylist's kitchen

by Clara Rodriguez Luboff

GATEHOUSE

To my husband David, for his constant
support; my daughters Sienna and Lia,
my two most honest fans; and my parents,
who taught me one of the most important
values in life: the importance of keeping a
balanced and positive relationship with food.

contents

introduction

I've been involved in a passionate love affair with food since the day I came into this world.

Born in São Paulo, Brazil, to my parents' (and grandparents') delight, my early years proved to be all about getting to know exciting new flavours and textures. There was nothing given to me that I refused to eat!

As far back as I can remember, all school holidays were spent at my grandparents' tropical beach house, located on a beautiful island off the coast of São Paulo. Their house rested under the shade of an enormous and luscious mango tree, and in the early months of the year – when the tree was producing at its maximum capacity – my cousins, siblings, and I used to help our grandfather pick ripe mangoes. After donating the tree's harvest to our neighbors and friends, we usually still had lots of leftover fruit, which would often be turned into jam, cake, juice – you name it! The aroma around that house and those unforgettable summer holidays will be stamped forever in my memory.

I knew I wanted to pursue a career related to food after spending countless hours interning in the test kitchen of *Claudia* magazine. At the time I was studying communications and advertising, and my knowledge of the professional food world was purely from observing and assisting, and from reading cookbooks.

When I turned 23, I decided to leave my corporate marketing job and spend a few months in Spain taking art, culinary, and marketing-related courses. While there, I met my husband, David, who was traveling around Europe at the time. A few months later I planned to visit him in Australia, and then never returned to live in Brazil full-time!

In 2000, David and I were lucky to be reposted to New York City for his job. It was there that I once again became immersed in cooking courses; I spent all my time learning as much as possible. When we returned to Australia in 2003, I decided to fulfill my biggest dream, which was to attend the Le Cordon Bleu international culinary school. I'm still thrilled to say that I graduated with a degree in culinary arts in 2004.

After graduation, I worked as a chef in various Sydney cafés, restaurants, and catering companies. I missed the more creative side of developing recipes, so I started applying for jobs at various publications. When I received a job offer from *Donna Hay Magazine*, I couldn't help but feel it was my dream coming true! There, I was exposed to Australia's food styling pioneer, Donna Hay herself, as well as magnificently professional food photography and stunning recipes. I left that position to pursue a freelance career in 2006, and have been doing what I love ever since.

Cooking fresh and tasty meals has always been my mission, but after moving to Singapore with my family in 2013, I took a close interest in wholesome recipes. The constant warm weather and outdoor lifestyle in this tropical country has definitely contributed to my culinary choices.

Living in Singapore has also brought me many new creative opportunities. One of them was enrolling in a wonderful photography course. Even though I still continue to learn every day, I am proud to say that I took the majority of the photos in this book.

Another opportunity I've had here is pursuing a different hobby of mine: pottery. For me, producing ceramic vessels is an extension of cooking, and it's very handy when I can use my creations to style food! Many of the ceramic plates and dishes in this book were handmade by me.

I'm captivated by the fascinating textures, flavors, and colors of ingredients, but cooking also takes me to a meditative space. I find the sizzling sound of garlic or onion cooking in a pan and the fragrance produced by each addition highly relaxing. Even though I love simply being in the kitchen, I do believe that every minute spent there should be spent wisely. Between juggling food styling jobs, looking after my kids, and making sure my house is functioning, my time cooking has had to be adapted to such a schedule. The recipes in this book are a reflection of my philosophy in the kitchen: creating meals and snacks that won't take all day to prepare, are packed with flavor, and, more importantly, that are wholesome.

I am delighted to be able to share some of my creations, recipes, food styling, and entertaining tips with you. I really hope I can inspire you and your family in future meals!

Clara

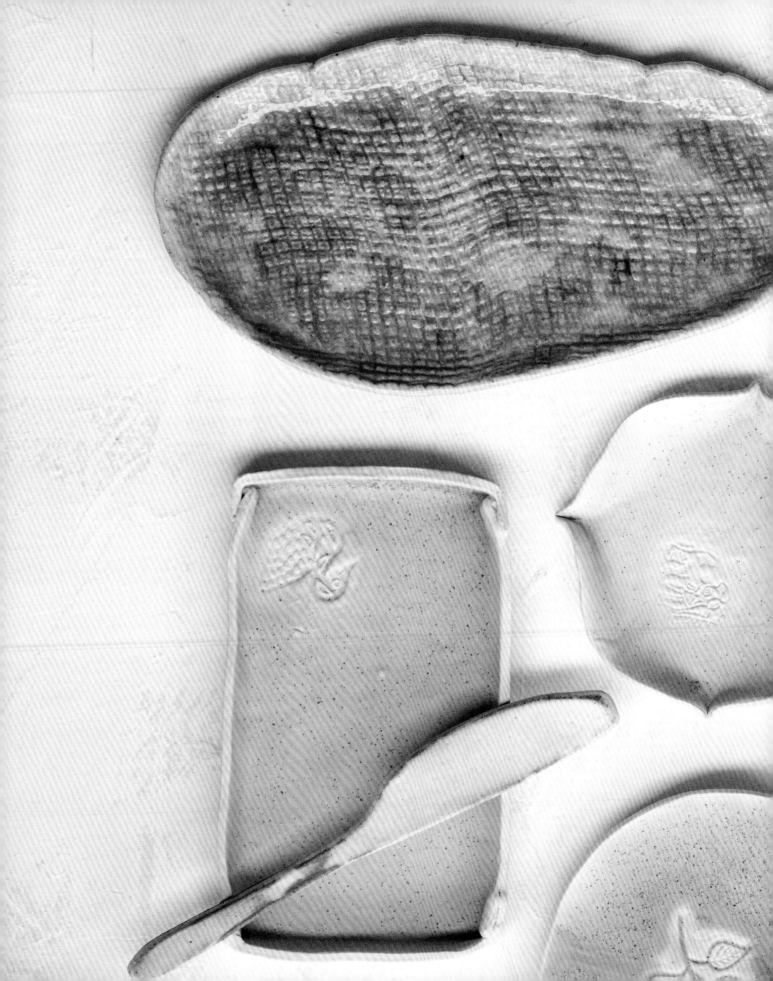

1

_{~~~~~~~~~~}

rise and shine

Like most other households, Monday through
Friday mornings at my place are synonymous
with a rush in preparation for school and work.
But since breakfast is my kids' favorite meal of the
day, it plays a special role in our lives. Though I'm
more of a savory person, my kids are prefer
to eat cereals, porridges, fruits, and smoothies.
In this chapter you'll find not only quick, practical
breakfast ideas, but also plenty of recipes to make
ahead as well as fantastic dishes to serve for a lazy
Sunday brunch.

coconut chia cups

papaya, mango, and almond smoothie

This smoothie is so simple yet so tasty, and it's especially great after exercising as it's cool and refreshing – not to mention nutritious. Sometimes I freeze the mixture into popsicle molds and turn it into a delicious afternoon treat for my kids after a long day at school.

 serves 2

1 small papaya, peeled, seeded, and chopped
1 large mango, peeled and chopped
1½ cups almond milk
2 tablespoons honey
Pinch of ground cinnamon

Place papaya, mango, almond milk, and honey in a blender and blend until smooth. Sprinkle with cinnamon to serve.

avocado and mint shake

There's nothing more refreshing to me than cold coconut water. But when you combine it with avocado, mint, and lime, it becomes a drink from the heavens that will keep you satisfied through to lunch – and it'll give you your dose of vitamin D for the day.

serves 2

1 medium avocado, halved and scooped
2 cups cold coconut water
¼ cup mint leaves
1 tablespoon maple syrup
½ tablespoon lime juice

Place all ingredients in a blender and blend until smooth. Serve immediately.

banana and blueberry smoothie

My kids are obsessed with this smoothie recipe, and they often don't want to start their day with anything else. We blend frozen bananas with frozen berries, yogurt, and honey, making what they call "healthy ice cream".

 serves 2

2 frozen bananas, chopped
1 cup frozen blueberries
2 cups yogurt of your choice
2 tablespoons LSA*
½ teaspoon ground cinnamon
2 teaspoons maple syrup or honey

* See glossary

Place all ingredients in a blender and blend until creamy and smooth. Serve immediately or store in freezer.

smashed avocado, chili, and lime toast

A typical Brazilian dessert is what we call "avocado mousse," which is avocado blended with milk and sugar and served with a few drops of lime juice on top. Back when I first moved to Australia, it didn't take me long to realize avocadoes were used in a completely different context. It took me a while to adjust to savory avocado recipes such as on toast for breakfast and in salads or salsas. Once I got used to it, though, I simply loved it (and still do!).

One of my favorite ways to eat avocado now is drizzled with lemon juice, extra virgin olive oil, sprinkled with red chili flakes, salt, pepper, and served with crunchy, healthy bread, like my maple and olive oil wholemeal loaf (see pg 35). Not only are avocadoes rich in vitamins B and K, but they also contain vitamins C and E, as well as potassium. The fruit does have a higher fat content than any other, but it's all good fat.

serves 2

2 small avocadoes, halved and scooped

2 tablespoons extra virgin olive oil

1½ tablespoons lemon juice

¼ teaspoon dry chili flakes

Sea salt and cracked black pepper, to taste

Place avocado halves on a serving plate. Drizzle with oil and lemon juice, and sprinkle with chili, salt, and pepper. Serve with toasted bread (use a fork to smash the avocadoes on top of each toast slice).

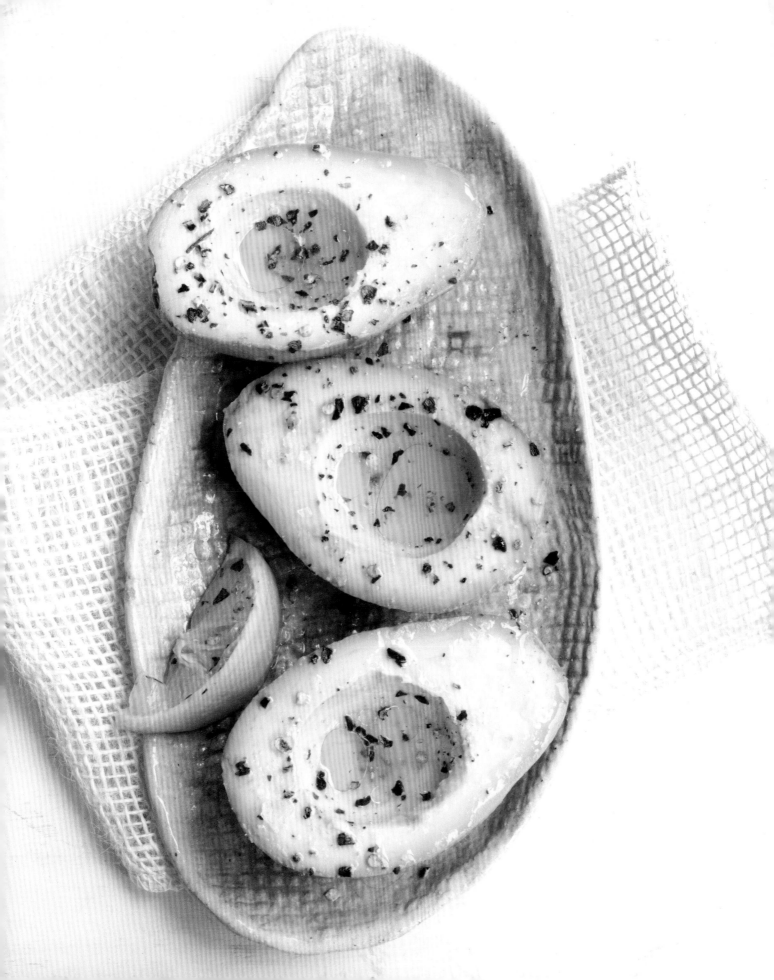

butternut squash soup with burnt butter and crispy sage

I still remember the Sunday night dinners at my Grandmother Celia's when she would make one of her specialties, sopa de milho verde *(corn soup with mustard greens and burnt butter). The soup was incredibly tasty, but the burnt butter was just the cherry on top of the cake! My kids love butternut squash, so I adapted my grandmother's recipe by changing the main vegetable here, still keeping the nutty butter flavor drizzled on top.*

serves 4–6

1 onion, roughly chopped
1 large leek, trimmed and roughly sliced
2 celery stalks, roughly chopped
2 carrots, peeled and roughly chopped
1.3lbs (600g) butternut squash, peeled, seeded, and roughly chopped
4 cups vegetable stock
6.5fl oz (200ml) coconut milk
Sea salt and cracked black pepper, to taste

In a large saucepan, place onion, leek, celery, carrots, squash, and stock. Over medium heat, bring the liquid to a boil, and then simmer, partially covered, for 25–30 minutes or until vegetables are soft. Allow it to cool slightly, and then blend until smooth. Return to pan, add coconut milk, and stir to combine, then season with salt and pepper to taste. Set aside and keep warm until ready to serve.

burnt butter and crispy sage

1 stick (100g) salted butter
½ cup sage leaves

Place butter in a small saucepan over medium heat. Cook for 2 minutes or until butter is melted and browned. Add sage and cook for an additional 1–2 minutes or until sage is crispy. Spoon burnt butter and crispy sage over soup to serve.

red lentil and cinnamon soup

I'm a huge fan of Middle Eastern spices and flavors like the ones in this Moroccan-inspired soup. This one-pot wonder is packed with protein, and it's filling and comforting, too. I often add a touch of chili flakes to mine, as well as a dollop of cooling Greek yogurt, to balance the flavors.

serves 4–6

1 tablespoon extra virgin olive oil
1 onion, finely chopped
4 garlic cloves, crushed
2 tomatoes, roughly chopped
3 carrots, peeled and diced
1½ cups dry red lentils
1 cinnamon stick
1 tablespoon tomato paste
8 cups vegetable stock
Sea salt and cracked black pepper, to taste
Cilantro (coriander) leaves, to serve

Heat oil in a large saucepan over medium heat. Add onion and garlic, and cook for 3–4 minutes or until onion is tender. Stir in tomatoes, carrots, lentils, cinnamon, tomato paste, and stock. Bring to a boil and cook, partially covered, for 20–25 minutes or until lentils are tender. Remove cinnamon stick, and season with salt and pepper to taste. Serve with a drizzle of olive oil and cilantro (coriander) leaves.

canja
(portuguese chicken soup)

~~~~~~~~~~~~~~~~~~~~~~~~~~~~~~~~~

Canja is one of those Brazilian recipes that is prescribed to anyone with a cold, a stomachache, or suffering a bad day (yes, it can make you feel better!), and it also works wonderfully as a casual Sunday night meal. I have put a few flavor twists on my grandmother's recipe by using brown rice instead of white and by adding cinnamon (a nontraditional ingredient), as I love the combination of this aromatic spice with chicken. It freezes really well, so make a large batch and keep some in the freezer for next week.

serves 6–8

1 tablespoon grape seed oil*	5 thyme sprigs
1 large yellow onion, finely chopped	1 cinnamon stick
4 garlic cloves, crushed	1 whole chicken
2 carrots, peeled and chopped	12 cups vegetable stock
2 celery stalks, finely chopped	¾ cup brown rice
2 ripe tomatoes, roughly chopped	Sea salt and cracked black pepper, to taste
2 tablespoons tomato paste	½ cup chopped green onions, to serve
2 bay leaves	Extra virgin olive oil, to serve

* See glossary

Heat the oil in a large saucepan over medium heat. Add onion, garlic, carrots, and celery, and cook for 6–8 minutes or until onion is tender. Add tomatoes, tomato paste, bay leaves, thyme, cinnamon, whole chicken, and stock. Cover with a lid, bring to a boil, then simmer over medium-low heat for 1 hour. Add rice and cook for an additional 30–35 minutes or until rice is cooked. Remove from the heat and allow to cool slightly. Remove chicken from the pan, discard skin and bones, shred meat, and return shredded meat to pan. Remove herbs and cinnamon stick, then season with salt and pepper to taste. Top with green onions and a drizzle of olive oil to serve.

shiitake broth with brown rice noodles

This comforting recipe is my vegetarian version of "chicken soup for the soul". The mushroom broth is rich and its flavor is full of depth, so it could easily be used as vegetable stock for risottos or stews.

 serves 8

12 cups water

1 10.5oz (300g) packet of dried shiitake mushrooms

4 garlic cloves, roughly chopped

1 large onion, roughly chopped

⅓ cup soy sauce

2 teaspoons sesame oil*

5.5oz (150g) brown rice noodles

½ cup chopped green onions, to serve

* See glossary

In a large saucepan, place water, mushrooms, garlic, onion, soy sauce, and sesame oil. Cover, bring to a boil, then simmer, partially covered, for 20 minutes over medium heat. Drain through a colander into another pot; discard the onion and garlic, but keep the mushrooms. Allow mushrooms to cool enough to handle. Remove mushroom stems, and then slice into strips. Return 2 cups of the mushrooms back into the pot. Add the noodles and cook for an additional 3–5 minutes or until noodles are tender. Top with green onions to serve.

macaroni and beans

~~~~~~

This is a healthier (and, in my opinion, much tastier) approach to traditional macaroni and cheese. It's still hearty, but this version is also packed with protein from the beans and nutrition from the vegetables.

serves 8

1 tablespoon extra virgin olive oil

1 white onion, finely chopped

4 garlic cloves, crushed

2 celery stalks, finely chopped

2 carrots, peeled and sliced

2 bay leaves

5 thyme sprigs

2 14oz (400g) cans white beans, drained

1½ cups macaroni

8 cups vegetable stock

Sea salt and cracked black pepper, to taste

Grated Parmesan cheese, to serve

Heat oil in a large saucepan over medium heat. Add onion and garlic and cook for 3–4 minutes or until onion is tender. Stir in celery, carrots, bay leaves, thyme, beans, pasta, and stock. Bring to a boil, and cook for 8–10 minutes or until pasta is al dente. Remove thyme sprigs and bay leaves, then season with salt and pepper to taste. Sprinkle with Parmesan cheese and a drizzle of olive oil to serve.

zucchini and carrot soup
with cheesy croutons

With or without the croutons, this simple zucchini (courgette) and carrot soup is perfect for cooler nights. My kids love dipping the croutons into the soup just like you do with a cookie dunked into a glass of milk.

serves 4–6

½ tablespoon grape seed oil*
1 white onion, roughly chopped
4 garlic cloves, roughly chopped
2 large green zucchinis (courgettes),
   roughly chopped
4 medium carrots, peeled and roughly chopped
4 cups vegetable stock
Sea salt and cracked black pepper, to taste

* See glossary

Heat the oil in a medium saucepan over medium heat. Add onion and garlic, and cook for 3–4 minutes or until onion is tender. Next, add zucchini (courgette), carrots, and stock. Bring to a boil, and then simmer, partially covered, for 15–20 minutes or until vegetables are soft. Allow to cool slightly, and then blend until smooth. Season with salt and pepper to taste. Set aside and keep warm.

cheesy croutons

2 tablespoons extra virgin olive oil
¼ cup finely grated Parmesan cheese
4 slices wholemeal sourdough bread,
   torn into small pieces

Preheat the oven to 350°F (180°C). Toss together oil, cheese, and bread pieces, and coat bread thoroughly. Place on a baking tray and bake for 15–20 minutes or until bread is golden and crunchy. Serve with zucchini soup.

zucchini, lemon, and date carpaccio

This carpaccio is a staple for when I entertain because it looks so impressively fresh. I normally arrange the thinly sliced zucchini (courgette) on a round platter with the pieces slightly overlapping each other. The zucchini slices must be paper thin, so the lemon juice from the dressing can get through and gently cook the zucchini, almost like a fish ceviche. The dates in the dressing add a lovely balance against the sourness of the lemon. It can be served as a side dish for roasted chicken, fish, or even as a stand-alone vegetarian meal paired with lentils and couscous.

serves 4–6

2 medium zucchinis (courgettes), sliced paper thin
1 small red onion, peeled and thinly sliced
½ cup mint leaves

Arrange zucchini (courgette), onion, and mint on a large platter and spoon over date dressing. Allow to marinate for 2–3 hours before serving.

date dressing

¼ cup lemon juice
¼ cup extra virgin olive oil
3 dates, pitted and finely chopped
¼ teaspoon dry red chili flakes
Sea salt and cracked black pepper, to taste

Place lemon juice, oil, dates, chili flakes, salt, and pepper in a bowl, and stir until well combined. Set aside, and spoon over carpaccio to serve.

watercress, smoked trout, and orange salad

I can't deny that I love mixing fruity and savory flavors together. The slight saltiness of the trout is perfectly balanced by the sweetness of the orange in this recipe, and the watercress adds a touch of natural pepper and a crunch to complement the other ingredients.

 serves 2–4

3 cups watercress leaves
1 small fennel bulb, thinly sliced
6oz (180g) asparagus, trimmed and blanched
2 oranges, peeled and sliced
5oz (150g) hot-smoked trout, flaked into chunks
⅓ cup pitted black olives
⅓ cup dill leaves
½ red onion, thinly sliced
1/2 cup mustard dressing (see pg 42)

In a salad bowl, toss together watercress, fennel, asparagus, orange, trout, olives, dill, and onion. Pour over mustard dressing to serve.

grape, mint, and halloumi salad

I grew up eating a type of white cheese called queijo branco, *and ever since I left Brazil, the closest cheese I've managed to find is Halloumi. It's saltier than* queijo branco, *so I normally like to balance its flavor by combining it with fruits such as cantaloupe, grape, watermelon, and pomegranate. Halloumi is best when grilled for a few minutes in a hot pan and eaten while still warm.*

serves 2

½ tablespoon extra virgin olive oil,
   plus 1 tablespoon extra for drizzling
6oz (180g) Halloumi, sliced into thin strips
2 cups seedless red grapes, halved
2 tablespoons slivered almonds, toasted
2 tablespoons sunflower seeds
¼ cup mint leaves
Dry red chili flakes, to serve (optional)
Lemon wedges, to serve
Sea salt and cracked black pepper, to taste

Heat oil in a nonstick frying pan over medium heat. Add Halloumi and cook for 1–2 minutes on each side or until cheese is golden.

To serve, toss together Halloumi, grapes, almonds, sunflower seeds, and mint. Drizzle with extra oil, sprinkle with chili flakes, add a squeeze of lemon juice, and season with salt and pepper.

crunchy lettuce with beetroot dressing and walnut dukkah

When I decided to try something new and make a salad dressing using earthy-sweet beetroot, it turned out absolutely delicious, and I knew I needed to show it off. Thus, I devised this recipe, where the dressing could really shine. The crunchy and spiced walnut dukkah adds great texture and lovely complementary flavor.

serves 4–6

5 baby heads of romaine lettuce, halved
¾ cup beetroot dressing (see pg 42)
¾ cup walnut dukkah (see below)
Sea salt and cracked black pepper, to taste
Crusty bread, to serve

Place romaine lettuce on a serving platter, drizzle with beetroot dressing, season with salt and pepper, and sprinkle with walnut dukkah (see below). Serve with crusty bread.

walnut dukkah

yields ¾ cup

½ cup walnuts, toasted
3 tablespoons sesame seeds, toasted
1 teaspoon ground cumin
1 teaspoon ground cilantro (coriander)
Sea salt and cracked black pepper, to taste

Place walnuts, sesame seeds, cumin, cilantro (coriander), salt, and pepper in the bowl of a mortar and pestle and pound until combined. (Alternatively, use a food processor and process until roughly chopped.) Keep in an airtight container for up to 1 month.

chopped chicken salad with curried tahini dressing

The curried tahini dressing really takes this chicken salad to the next level. The combination of macadamias, cranberries, tahini, and curry powder is unexpectedly delicious!

serves 4

4 cups romaine lettuce, chopped

4 grilled chicken breasts, roughly chopped

4 hard-boiled eggs, roughly chopped

1 avocado, halved, scooped, and diced

⅓ cup dried cranberries

½ small red onion, chopped

½ cup macadamias, roasted and roughly chopped

1 14oz (400g) can chickpeas, rinsed and drained

¾ cup curried tahini dressing (see pg 40)

Toss together lettuce, chicken, eggs, avocado, cranberries, onion, macadamias, and chickpeas. Pour over curried tahini dressing to serve.

pastel de palmito
(crunchy hearts of palm pastries)

This typical Brazilian street food is sold in open-air fresh food markets throughout the country and was a big part of my childhood. The fillings can vary between seafood, beef, or plain cheese, but this vegetarian version is my favorite.

 yields 25 pastries

½ tablespoon grape seed oil*, plus extra for
    deep-frying
½ onion, finely chopped
2 garlic cloves, crushed
1 14oz (410g) can hearts of palm in brine,
    drained and finely chopped
1 small tomato, finely chopped
1 tablespoon tomato paste
½ teaspoon dry oregano
¼ cup green onions, chopped
Sea salt and cracked black pepper, to taste
25 wonton wrappers*
¼ cup water mixed with 1 tablespoon of
    corn flour, for sealing pastries
Chili sauce, to serve (optional)

* See glossary

Heat oil in a medium saucepan over medium heat. Add onion and garlic, and cook for 3–4 minutes or until onion is soft. Add hearts of palm, tomato, tomato paste, oregano, green onions, salt, and pepper. Cook for 2–3 minutes or until the tomato is cooked, then remove from heat and allow to cool in the refrigerator.

Place wonton wrappers on a clean, flat surface. Place a teaspoon of the cooled vegetable mixture onto the center of each wonton. Use your finger to rub some of the water and corn flour mixture onto the edge of one half of the pastry, then fold to enclose. Use a fork to prick the edges of the pastry together to seal.

Heat oil in a medium frying pan over medium heat. Deep-fry pastries for 20–30 seconds on each side or until golden and crunchy. Drain on paper towel and serve with chili sauce.

beetroot and chickpea falafel

I often make a big batch of this beetroot and chickpea falafel and keep half in the freezer, so when I have a dinner party I can simply defrost and heat them up before serving. Tip: it pairs perfectly with za'atar labna (see pg 49).

yields 40 falafels

1lb (500g) chickpeas
1 large onion, roughly chopped
2 large garlic cloves, roughly chopped
½ cup mint leaves
1 teaspoon mild paprika
1 teaspoon ground cumin

1 large grated raw beetroot (about 2½ cups)
2 teaspoons baking powder
¾ cup wholemeal flour
Sea salt and cracked black pepper, to taste
2 tablespoons sesame seeds
Grape seed oil*, for shallow frying

* See glossary

Place chickpeas in a large bowl and cover with water. Allow to soak overnight. Drain chickpeas, discarding excess water. Place chickpeas, onion, garlic, mint, paprika, and cumin in the bowl of a food processor. Process until all ingredients are finely chopped. (Process in batches, if necessary.) Transfer mixture into a large bowl, then stir in grated beetroot. Add baking powder, flour, salt, pepper, and stir until well combined. Use your hands to roll tablespoons of the mixture. Sprinkle falafels with sesame seeds. Heat about an inch (2–3cm) of oil in a frying pan over medium heat. Shallow-fry falafel balls in batches for 5–6 minutes or until cooked through and golden. Drain on paper towel.

carne louca
(pulled beef salad in lettuce cups)

My grandmother had a wonderful domestic helper for more than 30 years, and she became part of our family. Geni was also an amazing cook, and many of my food memories from growing up are thanks to her. This recipe used to be one of her specialties, often served during our weekly family lunches.

Makes 20 lettuce cups

1lb (500g) beef brisket, fat removed
½ tablespoon grape seed oil*
Sea salt and cracked black pepper, to taste
½ small red onion, finely sliced
2 small ripe tomatoes, seeded and diced
¼ cup pitted black olives, roughly chopped
¼ cup parsley leaves, chopped
1 tablespoon extra virgin olive oil
1 tablespoon red wine vinegar
20 baby lettuce leaves

* See glossary

Preheat the oven to 300°F (150°C). Rub olive oil over brisket and season with salt and pepper. Heat a frying pan over high heat. Add brisket and cook for 3–4 minutes on each side or until browned. Place brisket on a baking tray and cover with aluminum foil. Slow cook in the oven for 2½ hours or until tender. Remove from the heat and allow to cool before shredding brisket into small pieces.

While the brisket cools, place onion, tomatoes, olives, parsley, olive oil, vinegar, salt, and pepper in a bowl. Add shredded brisket and toss until just combined. To serve, place lettuce leaves on a platter and spoon pulled beef salad onto each cup.

pao de queijo (brazilian cheese bread)

Pao de queijo *is a snack all Brazilians adore. It's available in every bakery across the country, and eaten not only for breakfast, but at any time of the day. This version is from my late Grandma Celia. Every time I had a sleepover at her house, I was greeted with these delicious treats for breakfast. The tapioca flour makes them wonderfully gooey in the inside. They are absolutely scrumptious!*

makes 15

3 cups tapioca flour*
1 cup full-fat, organic cow's milk
1 cup light olive oil
3 eggs
1 teaspoon salt
1½ cups Parmesan cheese, grated

* See glossary

Place tapioca flour, milk, oil, eggs, salt, and cheese in a bowl and whisk until well combined. Spoon mixture into a greased muffin tin until each hole is ¾ full. Bake for 20 minutes, or until golden and puffed. Serve warm.

polenta chips

These polenta chips are crunchy on the outside and creamy in the inside, but the best thing about them is that they are baked and not fried!

serves 4–6

4 cups vegetable stock
1 cup instant polenta
¾ cup Parmesan cheese, finely grated
2 tablespoons thyme leaves
Sea salt and cracked black pepper, to taste
1 tablespoon extra virgin olive oil

Bring stock to boil in a medium saucepan over medium heat. Add in polenta and cook for 2–3 minutes, stirring constantly, until thickened. Stir in cheese and thyme, then salt and pepper, to taste. Spoon mixture into a well-greased, 8in x 11in (20cm x 30cm) baking dish, and allow to set for 2–3 hours. Preheat the oven to 390°F (200°C). Slice polenta into sticks, toss with oil, and bake for 40–45 minutes or until golden and crunchy.

miang kham

This street snack of noodles wrapped in wild pepper leaves is one of my favorite starters when I go to a Thai restaurant. If you can't find wild pepper leaves, fret not: you can use lettuce leaves instead.

serves 4–6

12 wild pepper leaves*
3.5oz (100g) brown rice vermicelli noodles, soaked in boiling water until soft, then drained
½ cup Thai basil and ginger pesto (see pg 46)
1 long red chili, finely sliced, to serve
¼ cup green onions, finely chopped, to serve
¼ cup cashews, roasted and roughly chopped, to serve

* See glossary

To assemble the wraps, place pepper leaves on a serving platter. Toss noodles with pesto and divide evenly between each pepper leaf. Top with chili, green onions, and cashews.

Alternatively, place all ingredients in individual bowls and let your guests assemble their own wraps.

caprese bruschetta

This dish is a combination of pan Catalan from Spain and caprese salad from Italy. The colors and flavors of the mixed tomatoes and the bocconcini are a match made in heaven.

serves 4

8 slices wholemeal sourdough bread, toasted
1 large garlic clove, peeled and halved
1 small tomato, halved
1 cup mixed cherry tomatoes, halved
5oz (150g) baby bocconcini
⅓ cup basil leaves
1½ cups baby arugula (rocket) leaves
2 tablespoons extra virgin olive oil
1 tablespoon balsamic vinegar
Sea salt and cracked black pepper, to taste

Rub garlic and halved tomato onto each slice of toast. Place bread slices on serving plates. Top with cherry tomatoes, cheese, basil, and arugula (rocket). Drizzle with oil and balsamic, then season with salt and pepper to serve.

5

~~~~~~~~~~

high-protein mains

*I once read an article by a clinical psychologist about the powerful
emotional benefits that sitting down to a daily meal together as a family
has for children. I learned that this is not only important for our little
ones' self-esteem, but that it's also a long-lasting connection taking place
and opening very important communication channels between members
of the family. I know sometimes it's very tempting to just turn the TV on
and have our children eat in silence, but ever since I read that article,
I've been making the effort to have all devices off during a meal. At the
beginning my kids protested, but now they love it and really look forward
to it! I adapted the recipes from this chapter thinking about family
catch-up time, so that all meals can be prepared, marinated,
or cooked in advance for you and your family's benefit.*

fish soft tacos with apple salsa and smoked yogurt dressing

chili, coconut, and ginger baked salmon

This recipe is great for a tasty weeknight meal or for entertaining. It can be prepared a few hours beforehand and kept in the fridge until ready to be cooked. If you want to sub out salmon, any firm white fish would also work well here.

🥘 serves 6

2 cups coconut milk

¾in (2cm) knob of ginger, peeled and finely grated

1 long red chili, thinly sliced

4 green onions, thinly sliced

3 tablespoons soy sauce

2 tablespoons lime juice

6 x 7oz (200g) salmon steaks

Preheat the oven to 350°F (180°C). Place coconut milk, ginger, chili, green onions, soy sauce, and lime juice in a medium-size baking dish. Stir until combined and then coat fish. Bake for 15–20 minutes or until fish is cooked through. Serve with brown rice and steamed green vegetables.

fish soft tacos with apple salsa and smoked yogurt dressing

My kids love assembling their own food. I normally keep all the elements of this dish separated so it's easier for them to choose what they would like on their own tacos. I make another variation of this dish with sliced grilled chicken served with thinly sliced apples, shredded iceberg lettuce, cucumber, bell pepper sticks, and a quick lemon and olive oil dressing.

serves 4

fish

4 x 7oz (200g) white fish fillets, such as snapper, sole, or barramundi
½ tablespoon ground cumin
½ tablespoon ground turmeric
1 teaspoon dry red chili flakes (optional)
2 tablespoons grape seed oil*
Sea salt and cracked black pepper, to taste
2 cups shredded iceberg lettuce leaves
½ cup cilantro (coriander) leaves, to serve
8 soft wholemeal tortillas

* See glossary

Combine cumin, turmeric, red chili flakes, salt, and pepper, then season fish. Heat grape seed oil in a large nonstick frying pan over medium-high heat. Add fish in batches, and cook for 2–3 minutes on each side or until just cooked.

apple and chickpea salsa

1 red apple, diced
1 14oz (400g) can chickpeas, drained and rinsed
2 small cucumbers, peeled and diced
1 avocado, diced
½ small red onion, diced

Combine apple, chickpeas, cucumbers, avocado, and onion. Set aside until ready to serve.

smoked yogurt dressing

Juice of 1 large lime
¼ cup extra virgin olive oil
¾ cup plain Greek yogurt
1 teaspoon smoked paprika
1 teaspoon honey
Sea salt and cracked black pepper, to taste

Place all ingredients in a bowl, and stir until combined. Set aside in the refrigerator until ready to serve.

To serve, place all ingredients in bowls or platters in the center of the table, and let your guests or your family assemble their own tacos.

baked snapper

This has to be one of the easiest recipes in this book. Once the fish has been cleaned, scaled, and gutted by your fishmonger, all it takes is stuffing the ingredients into its belly cavity. It can be prepared in advance and baked just before serving. Guests often seem very impressed when they see a whole good-looking fish like this one on a platter. Little will they know it only took you minutes to prepare!

 serves 2

1 x 1.5lbs (650g) whole snapper
4 garlic cloves, roughly chopped
¾in (2cm) knob of ginger, sliced
1 cup Thai basil leaves*
Juice of 1 large lime
1 tablespoon extra virgin olive oil
Sea salt and cracked black pepper, to taste

* See glossary

Preheat the oven to 390°F (200°C). Place snapper on a baking dish. Open the cavity under the belly of the fish and insert garlic, ginger, and basil. Pour lime juice, oil, salt, and pepper over the fish. Bake for 20–25 minutes or until just cooked. Serve with crunchy salad and roasted veggies.

mediterranean fish parcels

The paper "bag" used to cook fish in this recipe acts as a steamer, locking all the flavors of the fish and the other ingredients inside. You could also make an Asian version by adding some soy sauce, grated ginger, sesame oil, shredded carrots, and bok choy to your fish.

serves 2

2 garlic cloves, crushed

2 tablespoons butter, softened

4 x 3.5oz (100g) firm white fish fillets such as snapper, sole, or barramundi

¼ cup pitted black olives

8 cherry tomatoes, halved

3.5oz (100g) baby corn, halved and steamed

Sea salt and cracked black pepper, to taste

Preheat the oven to 350°F (180°C). Place garlic and butter in a bowl and stir until well combined. Set aside. Cut two 15in (40cm) pieces of baking paper. Place 2 fillets in the center of each paper. Divide olives, tomatoes, and corn equally between each baking paper. Top with garlic butter mixture and season with salt and pepper. Fold paper to create a parcel, tucking the sides of the paper underneath each parcel to enclose. Place on a baking tray, and bake for 18–20 minutes or until fish is cooked through.

red curry chicken with lychee and spinach

I love the combination of sweet and savory elements in the same dish. The sweet lychees used here balance the spicy red curry and coconut cream in this Thai dish. Thai curry paste can be found in most supermarkets – I always look for the ones with no preservatives or flavor enhancers.

serves 4

1 tablespoon grape seed oil*
1 onion, finely chopped
4 garlic cloves, crushed
3 tablespoons Thai red curry paste
2 tomatoes, roughly chopped
2 cups (500ml) coconut cream
1 cup water
¼ cup fish sauce
1.5lbs (700g) chicken breast, thinly sliced
2 cups baby spinach leaves
1 14oz (400g) can lychees, drained

* See glossary

Heat a medium saucepan over medium heat. Add oil, onion, and garlic, and cook for 3–4 minutes or until onion is tender. Add red curry paste and cook for another minute. Add tomatoes, coconut cream, and water, bring to a boil, then simmer for 5 minutes. Add chicken, and cook for an additional 8–10 minutes or until chicken is cooked through. Stir in spinach and lychees and cook until spinach is wilted. Serve with steamed brown rice.

grilled rosemary chicken filets

This simple and quick recipe is a weekly staple at my home. Slice the chicken once it's grilled and toss it through salads or serve it up with some cauliflower and broccoli mash. The leftovers (if you have any!) can also be used in sandwiches or wraps.

serves 4

4 x 7oz (200g) chicken breasts, halved lengthwise
2 garlic cloves, crushed
2 tablespoons rosemary leaves, finely chopped
2 tablespoons extra virgin olive oil
Sea salt and cracked black pepper, to taste

Place all ingredients in a bowl and toss to combine. Allow to marinate for 2 hours or overnight. Heat a large nonstick frying pan over medium heat. Add chicken in batches, and cook for 3–4 minutes on each side or until cooked through.

moroccan-spiced roasted marylands

I love tossing together really tasty ingredients to make a simple yet super-yummy, one-pan meal. Here, I've used the Moroccan spice Ras El Hanout, which gives the chicken a beautiful cinnamon-like taste, not to mention the Middle Eastern aroma it produces around the house.

serves 4

6 x ½lb (250g) chicken Marylands (thigh and drumstick)
3 tablespoons extra virgin olive oil
1½ tablespoons Ras El Hanout*
1 large yellow onion, quartered
2 tomatoes, roughly chopped
4 baby eggplants, halved lengthwise
Sea salt and cracked black pepper, to taste

* See glossary

Preheat the oven to 350°F (180°C). In a bowl, toss chicken, olive oil, Ras El Hanout, onion, tomatoes, and eggplant. Place on a large roasting tray and season with salt and pepper. Roast for 45–50 minutes or until cooked through and golden. Serve with steamed couscous and roasted veggies or a crunchy salad.

za'atar roasted sweet potatoes

My kids love roasted sweet potatoes. Every time I make them, there's nothing left on the roasting tray. This recipe is super easy and can be prepared as a midweek side dish or as a healthy snack.

 serves 4

2 tablespoons grape seed oil*
4 medium sweet potatoes, peeled and sliced
   into ½in (about 1cm) thick
1 tablespoon za'atar*
Sea salt and cracked black pepper, to taste

* See glossary

Preheat the oven to 350°F (180°C). Toss oil and potato slices together to coat. Season with salt, pepper, and a sprinkle of za'atar. Place potatoes in single layers on two baking trays, and bake for 35–40 minutes or until potatoes are golden and crisp.

roasted brussels sprouts with mint yogurt

When I eat out and really enjoy my meal, I often create my version of the same recipe at home. This recipe was inspired by one of my favorite Middle Eastern restaurants in Singapore – Artichoke, from chef Bjorn Shen. I opted for roasting this very underestimated vegetable instead of deep-frying.

serves 4

1lb (500g) Brussels sprouts, halved lengthwise
1 tablespoon extra virgin olive oil
Sea salt and cracked black pepper, to taste
⅓ cup pomegranate seeds
¼ cup pine nuts, toasted
1¼ cups mint and yogurt dressing (see pg 39)

Preheat the oven to 350°F (180°C). Toss Brussels sprouts with oil and season with salt and pepper. Place on a roasting tray and roast for 25 minutes or until golden. Place roasted Brussels sprouts on a serving dish, top with pomegranate, pine nuts, and drizzle with mint and yogurt dressing. Can be served warm or cold.

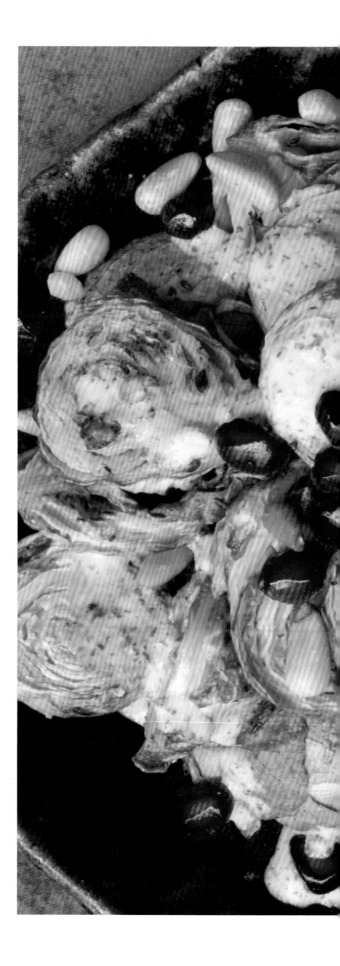

fennel and goat's cheese tart

This recipe makes two round tarts. If you only have one fluted baking tin, freeze the remaining pastry and fennel filling for another occasion. Alternatively, you can make one large tart using a large rectangular baking dish to feed a crowd. It's perfect to serve alongside one or more salads for a casual brunch or light dinner.

makes 2 tarts, 1 tart yields 4–6 slices

pastry

2 sticks (250g) salted butter, softened
1 cup plain flour
1 cup wholemeal flour
1 teaspoon sea salt
1 egg

Preheat the oven to 350°F (180°C). Place butter, plain flour, wholemeal flour, salt, and egg in a bowl, and use your hands to combine well, forming a smooth dough. Divide dough into two equal-size portions. Using your fingers, press dough into two 9in (23cm) round fluted tins. Use a fork to gently prick the base of the tart and bake for 12–15 minutes or until light golden brown. Remove from the oven and set aside.

filling

1 tablespoon grape seed oil*
1 onion, thinly sliced
2 medium fennel bulbs, trimmed and thinly sliced
1 teaspoon thyme leaves
Sea salt and cracked black pepper, to taste
7oz (200g) firm goat's cheese, sliced thinly
  (if using soft goat's cheese, crumble instead
  of slicing)
6 eggs
1½ cups cow's milk
½ cup finely grated Parmesan cheese

* See glossary

Heat oil in a large nonstick frying pan over medium heat. Add onion, fennel, thyme, salt, and pepper, and cook for 15–20 minutes, stirring occasionally, until fennel is tender. Set aside to cool slightly. In a bowl, whisk together eggs, milk, Parmesan, salt, and pepper. Divide fennel mixture between tart shells and top with sliced goat's cheese. Bake for 25–30 minutes or until set and golden.

7

~~~~~~~~~~

sweet cravings

*Like everything in life, I eat sweet foods
in moderation. What's more, when I prepare
desserts, I prefer to use non-processed, natural
sugar options such as maple syrup, xylitol*, dried
fruits, or honey. Some of the recipes from this
chapter are childhood favorites that I've adapted
to be a bit healthier, as well as very simple yet tasty
treats that are ready in a flash.*

* See glossary

chocolate chia mousse

cashew and chocolate truffles

I generally keep these truffles in my freezer for anyone in my family who is craving a little something sweet. They are light, nutritious, and just the right bite-size for a small indulgence.

Yields 40 truffles

1 7oz (200g) packet raw cashews
1½ cups semisweet chocolate chips, melted
2 medium ripe bananas, mashed
¼ cup raw cacao powder*, for rolling

* See glossary

Soak cashews in water for at least 4 hours or overnight. Drain and place in the bowl of a food processor. Process until finely chopped, then transfer into a mixing bowl. Stir in melted chocolate and bananas. Allow mixture to set in the fridge for 5 hours or overnight. Using wet hands, roll teaspoons of the mixture into balls and coat with cacao powder to serve. Store in the fridge for up to 2 days or in the freezer for up to 1 month.

blackberry and apple crumble

~~~~~~

Crumbles are very simple and versatile desserts to make as the fruit fillings can be made according to your own tastes. Here I've used blackberries and red apples (any red apple will do), but pears, blueberries, bananas, and strawberries are all fruits that work beautifully. Plus, it can be made ahead of time and baked while dinner is being served.

⌂ serves 4

3 (1.5 lbs; 650g) medium red apples, peeled, cored, and diced

2 cups frozen or fresh blackberries

½ cup brown or coconut sugar*

2 teaspoons vanilla extract

topping

½ cup brown flaxseed meal

1 cup baby (instant) oats

½ cup slivered almonds

½ cup brown or coconut sugar*

¾ cup coconut oil*

* See glossary

Preheat the oven to 320°F (160°C). Place apples, berries, sugar, and vanilla in a bowl and toss to coat. Divide into 4 individual baking dishes or one pie dish.

For the topping, place flaxseed meal, oats, almonds, sugar, and oil in a bowl and stir until combined. Spoon oat mixture over each individual dish and bake for 25–30 minutes or until top is golden and crunchy.

chocolate chia mousse

This mousse has to be one of the easiest desserts to make. On top of that, it tastes creamy and decadent, but in reality is good for you!

🍮 serves 6

2½ cups (600ml) coconut milk
½ cup water
¼ cup raw cacao powder*
⅓ cup maple syrup
½ cup chia seeds
Fresh raspberries or strawberries, to serve

* See glossary

Place coconut milk, water, raw cacao, maple syrup, and chia seeds in a bowl and whisk until cacao is dissolved. Pour into individual containers or a large serving bowl. Cover and refrigerate overnight. Serve with fresh raspberries or strawberries.

maple and banana
upside-down cake

My grandmother Stella used to make this cake often, complete with a sticky toffee sauce that covered the bottom of a cake pan. I decided to skip that step (and also cut the amount of sugar used in toffee) by simply substituting maple syrup. The flavor turns out exactly the same, and it has fewer calories!

serves 6–8

⅓ cup maple syrup
3 small bananas, sliced
2 sticks (200g) unsalted butter, softened
¾ cup brown or coconut sugar*
1 teaspoon ground cinnamon
2 teaspoons vanilla extract
3 eggs
1½ cups self-raising flour, sifted
⅓ cup full-fat organic cow's milk

* See glossary

Preheat the oven to 320°F (160°C). Pour maple syrup into an 8in (20cm) round cake tin that has been lined with baking paper. Place sliced bananas on top off the syrup and set aside. Place butter, sugar, and cinnamon into the bowl of an electric mixer and beat until mixture is light and creamy. Add vanilla and eggs, one at a time, beating well after each addition. Fold through flour, then the milk until just combined.
Spoon cake batter over bananas and bake for 45–50 minutes or until cooked when tested. Serve warm.

manjar branco (coconut flan with roasted plums)

You know you are Brazilian if you grew up eating manjar branco *at every family gathering. This dish is creamy, silky, and delicious. The sauce that complements it is traditionally made with dried prunes, but I like using fresh fruits whenever possible, so I gave it a try and used fresh plums. I'm pleased to say it turned out great!*

serves 6–8

2½ cups (600ml) full-fat organic cow's milk
2½ cups (600ml) coconut milk
½ cup corn flour
⅔ cup xylitol*
⅓ cup unsweetened coconut, shredded or flaked, to serve

* See glossary

Place cow's milk, coconut milk, corn flour, and xylitol in a medium saucepan over medium heat. Stir continuously for 10–12 minutes until mixture is bubbling gently and has thickened. Pour into a well-greased Bundt cake tin and refrigerate for 4–6 hours or until set.

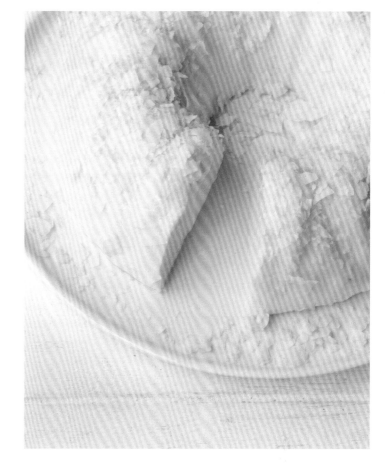

roasted plums

5 small plums, halved and pitted
¼ cup maple syrup
1 cinnamon stick

Preheat the oven to 350°F (180°C). Place plums in a small baking dish, add maple syrup and cinnamon, and roast for 20 minutes.

To serve, dip Bundt cake tin into a bowl of warm water for 1–2 minutes, then turn out onto a serving platter. Top with shredded or flaked coconut and serve with roasted plums.